1

To

_____

_____

From

_____

_____

Date

_____

Dear Gui:

This book is dedicated to you, and to all the children in the world.

Your great-great-grandmother wrote it when your great-grandmother was a child, like you, and was about to receive her First Communion. She wanted her daughter to know the meaning of "The Imitation of Christ", a beautiful book written in Latin by the friar Thomas ã Kempis over five hundred years ago.

I was also privileged to have had this companion in my childhood. It helped me to understand what the Child Jesus expected from me to be good and happy.

I hope you will keep this book as your companion, and allow its teaching to help you grow like a beautiful flower – a good and faithful Christian – in Child Jesus' garden.

With love,

Grandma Thaïs

The Imitation of Child Jesus

**A child's reading
of "The Imitation of Christ"**

Book I

My Spiritual Life

**Understanding What
Child Jesus Wants from Me**

Chapter I

Walk with Me and you will see a blue sky and a flowered path, says the Child Jesus. *Child, make sure that you always walk with your Sweet Child Jesus! Is it enough to know your Catechism by heart if you do not look for the love of Child Jesus?*

Meditation
There is nothing sweeter than pleasing Child Jesus. He is our best friend. Is it worth playing with friends and going on happy outings if we don't have the love of Infant Jesus? My Jesus, always give me the desire to imitate You now and forever.

What have I done lately to please Jesus?

_____

_____

_____

Chapter II

Children want to learn things. But what is learning without the love of God? It is a great wisdom to think well of others. If you see children doing something wrong, do not talk about them or judge yourself better. Pray for them.

Meditation

So many times, I have thought of myself as better than others! So many times, I have forgotten about my Child Jesus! Sweet Child Jesus makes my heart humble so I can someday sing joyful hymns to the Lord of Heavens.

What have I done lately to be as humble as Jesus?

_____

_____

_____

Chapter III

Only the truth pleases Child Jesus. And the truth is the Word of God: when Child Jesus spoke among the rabbis, His voice was strong because the Word of God calms the storms. Happy is the one who hears the Word of God.

Meditation

Whenever I want something from the world, I must find out if it pleases Child Jesus. Oh! Sweet Child Jesus, inspire me always with Your Holy Truth.

When have I felt inspired by the Holy Truth of Jesus?

_____

_____

_____

Chapter IV

Child, do not follow vain and bad advice, and do not allow yourself to be taken by the moment without first examining things carefully. Follow the advice of those older and wiser, those who love you and deserve your trust.

Meditation

It is hard and dangerous to judge my own affairs; therefore, I shall always look for advice and guidance in moments of uncertainty.

When have I followed the advice of my Mom, my Dad, or my teachers?

_____

_____

_____

Chapter V

Do not become sidetracked by focusing on how the Divine Mystery works. Do not try to find out what even the grown-ups cannot explain.

Meditation

I must learn to believe in the Divine Mystery of God as a truth. I believe in the Lord, my Sweet Child Jesus, as the most beautiful truth.

In my own words, how do I understand it?

_____

_____

_____

Chapter VI

Do not wish for the vanities of the world. What is the use of so many nice clothes and toys? Remember that Jesus was born in a stable and His bed was a manger of straw.

Meditation

Jesus was a poor child. I must think of the poor children and give them some of my toys. I will eat all that is given to me without complaining, because I know that there are children elsewhere dying of hunger. Lord, give me the desire to imitate You.

What have I done to help the poor?

_____

_____

_____

Chapter VII

Do not judge yourself better than your friends. Be humble in your heart, and you will please Child Jesus.

Meditation

So many times vanity causes a soul to stray! Child Jesus, keep vanity away from my heart!

When did I demonstrate that I am humble?

_____

_____

_____

Chapter VIII

Do not tell everyone what goes on in your little heart; choose to rely only on the people that are good and serve God.

Meditation

St. Paul said: *Our conversation is in Heaven.* I shall leave my feelings to meditation. We shall only have a deep familiarity with our Sweet Child Jesus.

How have I been trying to meditate and develop a dialogue with Child Jesus?

_____

_____

_____

Chapter IX

Jesus teaches us to obey. We must obey our parents, our teachers, and all authorities who are over us, especially when they are guiding us to the good and right ways of God.

Adam and Eve lost Paradise because they did not obey God. Child, be good and the Child Jesus will smile on you.

Meditation

Jesus obeyed His Father until death. Both Jesus and His Father are perfect! Although human beings are not perfect, I want to obey my Church, my parents, and my teachers whenever their actions and advice can guide me on the righteous path, so I can grow in wisdom, age, and grace.

Here is my obedience list:

_____

_____

_____

Chapter X

Do not talk too much, and before speaking, think about what you are saying, so you will only say what pleases Child Jesus.

Meditation

With all my heart, I wish to think before I say anything. Please help me my Child Jesus!

I want to say nice things such as:

_____

_____

_____

Chapter XI

To have peace in our hearts, we must have the ability to discipline our own silly demands and likings.

Meditation

Jesus expects me to forget all the unfairness of the world, and turn myself completely to Him, because only He is perfectly full of kindness and love. Child Jesus, make me deserve Your love.

I try to avoid my own silly demands such as:

_____

_____

_____

Chapter XII

During hard times, when working and studying, we shall think of Child Jesus, and we shall withstand all things for His love.

Meditation

Child Jesus also worked and helped His foster father St. Joseph. Child Jesus, give me courage to complete the tasks that I have already been given to perform in this world.

Things I have done to help at home:

_____

_____

_____

Chapter XIII

We will meet people who will try to give us bad advice. The bad angels do not sleep and are always trying to make us fall into temptation. We must pray a Hail Mary, with much faith, and the Mommy of our Dear Friend will ask Her Son to help us.

Meditation

The Saints were also tempted, and resisted. Child Jesus, keep in me the desire to resist temptations.

Something that the bad angels wanted me to do but that I resisted:

_____

_____

_____

Chapter XIV

Do not judge your friends by their doings. Remember, many times appearances are wrong. But if they do something wrong, remember that you are not the one to judge them.

Meditation

Each person must answer God individually for his or her actions. Child Jesus, give me repentance for my mistakes and the ability to forget the mistakes of other people.

I did not judge my friend when:

_____

_____

_____

Chapter XV

Giving alms is charity, and that makes Child Jesus happy. But giving them alone is not enough; we must give with our hearts too. We can also be charitable with words and friendly gestures. And sometimes, if we cannot do much, our hearts suffer – we suffer for charity.

Meditation

"Alms do not come from the hands only, but also from the heart." Child Jesus, give me a good heart, today and forever. Amen.

I am kind and charitable when:

_____

_____

_____

Chapter XVI

Suffer with resignation if someone hurts you. Remember that you also have hurt others.

Meditation

Child Jesus, the most perfect One suffers without complaining over our mistakes. My dear Child Jesus, make me strong to stand any harm that may reach me.

When I hurt someone I try to make up for it. Example:

_____

_____

_____

Chapter XVII

Serve God, be good, and you will please Child Jesus.

Meditation

Guy de Fontgalland and Anne de Guigné[1] knew how to love Child Jesus. I wish I can love You as much!

I please the Child Jesus when I:

_____

_____

_____

1 Saint children, living example of what the love of God and the Eucharist can bring to a child's heart. Examples of devotion, generosity and love. Guy de Fontgalland (1913 -1925) Anne Gigné (1911-1922)

Chapter XVIII

The Martyrs were so sublime in their love for God...
innocent virgins, children, devoted men; they were
all sacrificed for their will to follow the steps of
Christ.

Meditation

I have done no sacrifice for Child Jesus. My Sweet
God, strengthen my soul so I can suffer for Your
love.

For the love of Child Jesus, I will sacrifice my:

_____

_____

_____

Chapter XIX

We must pray every day and ask Child Jesus to give us Faith, because Faith is a weapon to defend ourselves from the bad angels.

Meditation

From the time of our birth, we hurt and feel deceived. Prayer is the remedy of the soul. My Child Jesus, never let me forget to pray.

I will write here how many prayers a day I will say from now on:

_____

_____

_____

Chapter XX

Play because you are a child. But you already have understanding, so avoid bad games. What is the use of all the toys and games in the world if you are not kind? Do not demand too much of your parents. Child Jesus played with small pieces of wood left over from His foster daddy's carpentry.

Meditation

Toys get broken; time goes by, only the smile of Child Jesus remains in eternity. Oh, Child Jesus, give me Your smile forever.

I will be happy with the toys I have. I will wait until my parents can buy me …

_____

_____

_____

Chapter XXI

When Jesus was born, He received offerings from the Three Kings and shepherds. You should also go to the Nativity and offer the joy in your child's heart to Child Jesus.

Meditation

Unlike the Three Kings, I do not have myrrh, incense, or gold to offer Child Jesus, but I do have the joys of my child's heart, and I will offer them all to Him.

I have the following beautiful feelings in my heart that I want to offer Jesus:

_____

_____

_____

Chapter XXII

Do not believe that your friend is happier than you just because he has better clothes, a nicer home, and more money. True happiness is only for the ones that have Child Jesus in their hearts.

Meditation

Happy is the one that has a healthy mind and a good heart: Child Jesus, give me these blessings!

I don't envy my friend for having…

_____

_____

_____

Chapter XXIII

Think about your future, child. Practice all the good you can. You are a little one today, but tomorrow you will be a grown-up. Our actions grow with us. If you identify yourself with evil, even if you do not want to become evil, you will be evil. In the same way, the good that you try to spread will always grow and be with you.

Meditation

I shall not forget that I will be a grown-up someday. I want to grow in wellness and love for my God. Oh, Lord, make my wish steady throughout my life.

When I grow up, I want to become a _____

_____ in the service of God.

Chapter XXIV

You shall love your God first, and then your parents. Do not wish evil to anyone and do not envy whatever your friends have. Go to Church and pray. Go to the Nativity, smile at Child Jesus, and ask your Guardian Angel to guide you always.

Meditation

Child Jesus is very patient and waits for me; however, I must not make Him wait. I must seek Him.

Child Jesus, I want to be good and make You smile. When I go to church, I will promise You that:

_____

_____

_____

Chapter XXV

Child Jesus has His flock of little sheep. Whenever one strays, He will be sad and waiting for his or her return, but when they return, He will welcome them and there will be joy in Jesus' heart. Nevertheless, some little sheep never stray away from His steps, and you, dear child, should be among those. Do not ever stray away from Sweet Child Jesus.

Meditation

I always want to please my friends, and I never intend to hurt them. How about my best friend Sweet Child Jesus? How could I dare to hurt Him?

Child Jesus, bestow on me, always, the desire that I have now of never offending You, pleasing You always, and loving You a lot.

Amen.

My Notes

My Commitments

My Pictures

Place your photo here

My Pictures

Place your photo here

Place your photo here

My Pictures

Place your photo here

Place your photo here

Place your photo here

Published by Translations Decoder LLC
Centennial, CO, USA 2015
www.translationsdecoder.com
ISBN-13: 978-0996956307
(My Spiritual Life)
ISBN-10: 0996956301

This book was translated and adapted from Iris Fróes, *A Imitação do Menino Jesus*, 1935, Rio de Janeiro, Brazil, 1st edition. All Brazilian editions of this book received a Roman Catholic Church *Nihil Obstat*.

Disclaimer

This book is meant to supplement, not replace, the Roman Catholic Catechism. The publisher advises parents and educators to take full responsibility orienting children for their understanding and to knowing their limits. Before practicing the skills described in this book, be sure that children do not take risks beyond their experience, aptitude, training, mental and emotional comfort level.

Although the publisher has made every effort to ensure that the information in this book was correct at press time, the publisher does not assume and hereby disclaims any liability to any party for any loss, damage, or disruption caused by errors, omissions, or interpretations, regardless of cause.

Author Iris Fróes

1902 – 1975

Brazilian writer, poet and journalist.

Translator Thaïs Lips

Thaïs, the granddaughter of author Iris Fróes, is an English, Portuguese, French, and Spanish translator. She attended law school in Brazil, has a Certificate of Proficiency in English from the University of Michigan, and a Teaching English as a Second Language certificate from the University of Colorado in Denver. She lives in Denver, CO, where she is currently the president of the Colorado Translators Association. She has lived in Brazil, England, Wales, France, and Oman.

Acknowledgment

Dr. Spencer Thomason, my dearest friend Gus, an early childhood educator, among other things, who helped me to make my grandmother's work a reality in the 21st century.